£250

Lytham and St Annes

The Reluctant Resorts

by

Kath Brown

Lancashire County Books

Lytham and St Annes

The Reluctant Resorts

by

Kath Brown

Lancashire County Books, 1992

ERRATUM
The publishers would like to point out that the captions
for the two bottom pictures on page 26 have been
transposed by mistake.

Lytham and St Annes: The Reluctant Resorts
by Kath Brown

Text copyright, © Kath Brown, 1992

Published by Lancashire County Books, 143 Corporation Street, Preston, 1992.

Typeset by Carnegie Publishing Ltd., Preston

Printed by the Bath Press, Bath, Avon

British Library Cataloguing-in-Publication Data
A CIP record for this book is available from the British Library.

ISBN 1-871236-21-5

Contents

'The very sweetness, vigour, and picturesqueness of the town and its surroundings seem refreshing even to write of it.'

Dr Poole in his book 'Lytham'. (Corporation Guide series, London, 1909.)

Preface

I was asked to assemble the following work as a way of publicising photographs in the Local History Collection held at St Annes Central Library. I do not profess to be an expert on the history of Lytham St Annes, rather an interested amateur, and this is not intended as a scholarly tome. I am well aware that this book leans very heavily on the history of St Annes on the Sea rather than Lytham, but this reflects the contents of the collection as well as my own personal knowledge of the area.

Finally, I have tried to show something of the battle of wills between various factions in the towns, some trying to establish and publicise them as holiday places, others determined to maintain their residential charm.

Kath Brown, 1 July 1992

Lytham and St Annes: an introduction

'I commend this place to harassed businessmen, as from my own experience I believe it will prolong their lives and enable them to do a great deal more work than would be possible under other conditions.'

Charles Macara talking of St Annes after the Improvement Act developments of 1914. From the St Annes on the Sea Express, *29 May 1914*.

T he origins of the English seaside resort lie in the fashion for sea-bathing which developed in the late eighteenth century. Whereas previously the wealthy visited spa towns, they now travelled to coastal hamlets in search of the 'cure'. Before the mid eighteenth century doctors had recommended taking the mineral waters at spas, but after this time they believed that by both immersing oneself in, and drinking, sea water, a body could be returned to health. Sea-bathing, as the immersion in sea water came to be known, was the preserve of the very rich. Only they could afford to travel any distance in those days, always by private coach and horses. In this way, Lytham was transformed into a seaside resort and visited by a wealthy class before holidaymaking became a national institution. According to 'Geoffrey Gimcrack', recording life in Lytham in 1822, 'many of the nobility and gentry make it a rule to visit there during the months of May, June, July and August, and even in September and October, which are deemed the cool months for visiting the seaside'.[1]

Before the gentry began to visit the seaside, Lytham existed as a fishing and farming village, its inhabitants surviving by 'getting muscles [sic], cockles, etc.'[2] or by working as labourers or tenant farmers.

The arrival of the moneyed visitors created a need for service industries – accommodation, places to eat, entertainments and places for visitors to spend their money. Over the next 100 years, Lytham expanded to meet these demands.

There is no doubt that the success of the holiday industry in Lytham was due in no small part to the entrepreneurial skills of the Clifton family. They were responsible for the particular tone of the resort and were careful to cultivate the best image for their town. They also built hotels and inns there.

In contrast, St Annes, born after the development of the sea-bathing craze, was created by men of vision with the holiday industry in mind. In 1874, Elijah Hargreaves, a wealthy east Lancashire landowner, after taking a morning stroll between Lytham and Blackpool, decided to lease 600 acres of barren land from the Clifton estate office. A man of tremendous enterprise, he had long contemplated developing a health resort of his own. That he managed to turn what was largely sandhills into a flourishing and prosperous resort is testimony to his great foresight. He formed the St Annes on the Sea Land and Building Company, named after the parish church of St Anne, built by Lady Eleanor Cecily Clifton a year earlier to serve the workers of the hamlet of Heyhouses. The town took the name of St

Annes on the Sea as a result.

The Company was responsible for much of the early development of St Annes. Men of the Company, many of them east Lancashire businessmen like Hargreaves, made decisions as to how the town should progress. Although less upper-class than their Lytham contemporaries, there is little doubt that they aspired to an exclusive resort. By about the time that St Annes began to develop, though, travel had been opened up to the lower classes by means of the railway. Now health resorts were not the sole preserve of the very rich; a different type of holidaymaker had appeared. Never sure of which type of tourist it wanted to attract, the town attempted, in turn, to entice both the sophisticated visitor and the ordinary holidaymaker.

Although both towns developed very differently, even from their earliest existences as resorts they experienced similar dilemmas as to how they should grow. Whilst enjoying the patronage of wealthy and influential visitors in the beginning, they eventually had to choose whether to maintain their exclusive image or learn to please a new breed of holidaymaker at the expense of that image, as neighbouring Blackpool had done. As a result, while they were deciding which way to develop, they became 'reluctant resorts', wanting to please both visitor and resident alike.

1. G. Gimcrack, *Lytham in 1822* (by a correspondent to the Babbler) in P. Whittle, *Marina* (Author, n.d.) p. 26.
2. Ibid, p. 28.

Bathing machines on St Annes beach. These were transported into the water by horses. Bathers were obliged to change in them, and emerged into the sea a safe distance from spectators on the beach. Lytham had only three machines in 1820, which doubled as carriages for churchgoers on wet Sundays.

In the early 1800s Lytham was the premier resort on the Fylde coast; about one-third again bigger than Blackpool. But Lytham steadfastly refused to accept the working-class holidaymakers who flocked to Blackpool in the 1870s, and maintained its image of gentility and decorum.

That Sea-bathing Craze

Sea-bathing was something of an ordeal in the early days. Although there are earlier recorded instances of men swimming naked a short distance from the shoreline, bathing was normally carried out from a 'bathing machine', a wheeled compartment in which bathers could change into swim attire. This was pulled into the water, usually by one or two horses, to a depth where bathers could emerge into the sea, supposedly unseen by spectators. An attendant, usually female, was always at hand to help the ladies, and often the gentlemen too. It was the duty of the attendant to push the bather under the waves to ensure he or she obtained the full benefit of the 'water cure'. Bathing attire in the early 1800s was little less than normal daywear; the ladies were expected to keep on their corsets and often their hats, even in the water. Later in the century women became a little more adventurous and raised their skirts to ankle height in order to paddle in the sea. Nevertheless, photographs taken as late as the 1920s show that, even in the hottest months, the crowds of holidaymakers – even children – wore heavy clothing, with hats and long skirts for the women being *de rigeur*.

At a time when the credibility of a coastal resort was measured by the number of bathing machines it possessed, Lytham was found to be a little lacking. 'The bathing vans were still unequal to the

Paddling at St Annes. The new resort, though not as staid as its neighbour, Lytham, still adhered to the bathing norms; hats and long skirts, even on the hottest days, were de rigeur for the women right up to the early 1920s.

Donkeys on St Annes beach. There is no clear explanation as to how the tradition of donkeys on the sands originated, though early coastal resorts staged horse races on the sands and promenades at certain times of the year. This was certainly true of Lytham; John Clifton, a great supporter of racing, organised a horse race every Whit holiday. Donkey races may have been adapted from these early horse races, though they could also have been introduced by gipsy traders.

St Annes beach in about 1910. Developments on the promenade have begun, with the addition of the bandstand and shelters. There are donkeys, and some beach vendors.

Two photographs showing the extent to which Lytham developed its beach for the recreation of its holidaymakers. The swings and roundabout were its answer to the beginnings of Blackpool's pleasure beach, but it never stooped to gipsy fortune tellers and funfairs.

as it was for bathing.

Despite the machines, breaches of bathing conduct were commonplace in Lytham. A letter to the *Preston Chronicle* in 1826 berated the lack of any bathing rules and complained of men 'most shamefully exposing their persons to the great annoyance of females'.[2] It seems strange to hear of such conduct in sedate Lytham, even in those times, especially since Southport, a contemporary resort, apparently did have regulations; men were not allowed to bathe within 100 yards of female bathing machines there and also were restricted from bathing within a given distance from the beach in order to protect the ladies' decency.

The mid nineteenth century saw a change in attitude towards sea-bathing. The development of the railways opened up the established resorts to the lower classes. The closure of the mills at Whitsuntide and 'Wakes Weeks' brought

demands on their accommodation and many people were compelled to dispense with their decorous shelter and unrobe themselves on the more secluded parts of the beach.'[1] In fact, originally, Lytham had only three bathing machines, one owned by a Mr Parkinson and the other two by Mr George Gillat, 'both of whom, from long experience and constant practice, are declared to be particularly adroit in delicately handling the fair females out of the machines into the water'. The machines doubled up as carriages on wet Sundays to convey people to church, and it is thought that demand was as much for this service

increased leisure time to the Lancashire working classes and this, combined with a rising standard of living, enabled them to take regular summer holidays. The Bank Holidays Act of 1871, passed only four years before the foundation of St Annes on the Sea, also brought more free time to a class which wanted to enjoy its new freedom. Doctors' opinions were changing, too. Whereas previously bathing in sea water had been advocated as a cure-all, now a considerable number of physicians were promoting the idea that sunshine and sport were a form of preventive medicine and therefore it was no longer just the

Ansdell and Fairhaven developed even later than St Annes on the Sea. While following a similar pattern of development to St Annes, they retained their individual atmospheres and never achieved a very large tourist season.

'invalids' who could benefit from the resorts: the healthy and the active could do so, too. A new brand of tourist descended on the resorts; these were the 'holidaymakers', demanding different types of entertainment, a more liberal attitude to bathing and cheaper accommodation. Released from the grime and noise of a factory or mill for a week or a few days, they had little time for the airs and graces of a pompous watering place. What Lytham, and later St Annes, refused to give to the new holiday class, Blackpool took on board with enthusiasm. As a result, while Lytham and St Annes managed to retain their upper-class images as watering places for the wealthy, even to the point of dissociating themselves completely from Blackpool, the latter prospered financially, quick to avail itself of a lucrative business venture.

The rise of Blackpool from a small resort into a great holiday centre was dramatic. In 1863 the first Blackpool Pier was built, a year before Lytham's. Not afraid to capitalise on its popular, if vulgar,

pursuits, Blackpool actively promoted its fortune tellers and funfairs. The promenade at Blackpool was developed for the working class, with vendors of cheap goods and sideshows in proliferation. The residents of Lytham abhorred this and steadfastly refused to change.

What happened in the next few years was not so much the further development of Lytham, but its determination to remain as it had started, a place for the prosperous to enjoy the dignity and grandeur of yesteryear.

When St Annes was created a few years after Blackpool's rise to fame, it developed on different lines. It, too, grew into a middle-class resort, shunning the Blackpool crowds and the garish amusements. Although very different from Lytham in appearance and in character, the two towns shared a desire to remain 'respectable'.

1. John Porter, *The History of the Fylde in Lancashire* (W. Porter & Sons, 1876), p. 443.
2. Letter to the *Preston Chronicle*, 13 Sept. 1826, in P. Whittle, *Marina*, p. 30.

In Plush Surroundings: hotels and inns

Seaside resorts were built around the hotels and inns which accommodated the temporary guests who had come for sea-bathing. There is little doubt that the quality of the first hotels influenced the later developments in the town.

Many inns and hotels in Lytham were owned and built by the Clifton family. This is not surprising, considering that not only did the Cliftons own all the town in the late eighteenth century, but they also leased land to tenants on very restrictive terms. Any buildings erected on land leased from the family could only be then sold with their permission. Therefore, there was no incentive to build outside the family.

The first hotel, the Wheat Sheaf, was erected in Clifton Street in 1794. Built where the Post Office is now, it was managed by a Mr Crookall. The Clifton Arms Hotel was established a couple of years later, in 1796, on the opposite side of the road to the Wheat Sheaf, facing the sea. There were less salubrious surroundings to

be had, if money was short, suggesting that Lytham had not yet closed its doors to the poorer visitor. According to Baines' *History and Directory*, written in 1825, 'Accommodation is to be had here of all sorts, from the highest to the most humble, regulated by the charge, and by other circumstances'.[1] As well as the two large hotels, the Commercial Inn and the Ship Inn offered cheaper board and lodgings, and rooms could be had, with enterprising local families looking to supplement their income during the summer months. Charges varied considerably. Baines mentioned that 'At the Clifton Arms, the charge for board and lodging, exclusive of wine and liquors, is seven shillings per day in private, and six shillings in public; at the Commercial Inn, the charge is 5s. 6d. and at the Ship Inn, 3s. 6d. per day for board and lodgings'.[2] One way or another, profits found their way to the Clifton coffers. The Commercial Inn mentioned by Baines was built just behind another hotel, the Market

Lytham Square in about 1850. Williams Deacons Bank, on the right, was the site of the original Wheat Sheaf, the first hotel in Lytham. The Ship Hotel is on the left. Later, the more expensive hotels were positioned opposite the promenade, facing the sea front, and away from the town centre itself.

The Ship Hotel, Lytham. Built on the site of two taverns, this hotel still retains its magnificent structure today. In 1825 it offered board and lodgings for 3s. 6d. per day.

Hotel, now the County. The Ship Inn replaced possibly two other taverns.

These were the first buildings established to meet the needs of the holiday trade, the Wheat Sheaf and the Clifton Arms being the superior establishments. In 1839 a new Clifton Arms was built on its present site, opposite the promenade and green at Lytham. It began to enjoy a reputation, not only for its pleasant surroundings, but also for its wonderful service and excellent views. An anonymous traveller staying there in the late nineteenth century claimed, 'We were ushered into the travellers' room in such a pretty manner that, we are sure, bespoke all that urbanity of true English feeling, which must gain the approbation of all who look for good manners and genuine hospitality . . . this is sweet accommodation to the visitor'.[3] The whole layout of the town was changing to accommodate not only visitors, but residents too. The larger hotels were

developed away from the main thoroughfares and placed outside the centre along the promenade, facing the green. The Neptune Hotel, built in 1854 and later called the Queens (1860), was erected along the same front. These hotels were intended to display the opulence and wealth of the town. They were show places established on prime sites and were very definitely hotels, not inns. Those inns of the past, along with boarding houses and cheap entertainment, were by now strictly for Blackpool.

Hotels in St Annes helped to establish the aura of that town, too. The St Annes Hotel was the first building, apart from shanty huts for the construction workers, to be erected by the St Annes on the Sea Land & Building Company. Built in 1875, it was only the second building of any consequence in the town; the first being the parish church of St Anne, established in 1873. This hotel played a key role in the history of St Annes; many plans for the

Queen's Hotel, Lytham

Originally called the Neptune Hotel, this hotel was built in 1854, changing its name to the Queens in 1860. Like the Clifton Arms Hotel, it was erected along the sea front facing the green and promenade, and looking out towards the sea.

development of the town were created within its walls as the Land & Building Company met there often. It was also used as a club house by the Lytham and St Annes Golf Club at the beginning of that institution's history – a special room was put aside by the proprietor, A. J. Holloway, until 1897 when the club established its own clubhouse on the course itself. It was a prominent landmark for the town. It was managed initially by Mr Richard Cookson of Lytham. He was followed by a succession of proprietors, including Mrs Ricketts, the sister of Mr Thomas who laid out the Ashton Gardens and those on the promenade. The hotel was demolished in the late 1980s and replaced by the St Annes Tavern.

The Grand Hotel and Victoria Hotel, both erected in 1897, were situated a good distance away from the St Annes Hotel site, but together the three established themselves as the big hotels in the town.

When the Imperial Hydro was beginning to be developed in 1908, several reports stated that these were the only hotels in St Annes. This is somewhat misleading. Although they were certainly the major establishments, other guest accommodation was available. Many families, as in Lytham, 'took in' visitors to stay and provided lodgings for small numbers of holidaymakers. The lists of visitors, regularly printed in the local papers in 1905 and 1906, show that they came from as far away as Birmingham and Sheffield as well as from inland Lancashire towns such as Manchester and Bury. A few boarding houses were advertised in the press, one rejoicing in the name of 'Mussoorie Boarding House' and there were a couple of 'hydros' – the South Down Hydro, now the St Annes Town Hall, and the Dunes Hydro, on Clifton Drive South, later converted into flats. These hydros should not be confused with

An early postcard showing the St Annes Hotel, the first building to be erected by the St Annes on the Sea Land & Building Company in 1875. That it was the first building emphasizes the positive attitude towards tourism that the early pioneers of the town supported.

St Annes' impressive Grand Hotel, built in 1897. It benefited greatly from the development of the new Esplanade Gardens in 1914, which considerably improved the view from its sea-facing windows.

the Imperial Hydros later built in Blackpool and St Annes. Rather they were a type of boarding house, catering for a class of people less wealthy than hotel guests. An early advertisement for the South Down Hydro describes a 'comfortable boarding house, with billiards, smoke and recreation rooms and late dinners'.[4] They did not attempt to attract a particularly wealthy clientele, but were positioned in strategic places, along the tram route and close to the sea front. As St Annes expanded and became more upmarket, the hydros declined in significance.

Hotels were important in establishing and maintaining the personality of both towns. Lytham's early inns were replaced by grander hotels as the town fought to protect its superior image. St Annes, initially not too sure which way it should develop, established grand hotels *and* boarding houses until it chose to maintain its exclusivity and eventually moved away from the boarding house image. The foundation of St Annes' impressive, yet monstrous, Imperial Hydro, mentioned in the next chapter, says more about that town's changing attitude to the holiday trade than any of the establishments mentioned here. What did become important to both Lytham and St Annes was the need to please the residents as much as the tourist. Hotels had to be part of the residential character of the towns. By and large, most of the hotels did conform well to the architectural character of the resorts. They were large but tasteful, to reflect the affluence of the residents, and thereby the visitors they desired to accommodate.

1. E. Baines, *History, Directory and Gazetteer of the County Palatine of Lancaster*, vol. 2 (Wales & Co., 1825), pp. 54–5.
2. Ibid, p. 55.
3. *History of Lytham* in P. Whittle, *Marina*, p. 76.
4. *Lytham Times*, 7 Apr. 1898, p. 2.

The Hydropathic Experience

By the early 1900s, hydropathic establishments, or hydros for short, had become fashionable in coastal resorts. The Imperial Hydro in Blackpool was already earning dividends of 12½% for its shareholders in 1908. The hydros were hotels, usually expensive, which offered several types of medicinal water treatment. In effect, they were the forerunners of health farms, combining relaxation in the mild climate with restorative tonics. Being coastal, the hydros made use of the available sea water for their 'remedial baths' as well as the pleasant surroundings of their holiday resort for recuperation. In 1908 the prospectuses for both the Imperial Hydro at St Annes and the Norbreck Hydro at Blackpool were issued. The trend had been well established. In a sense, hydros were giving the service for which seaside resorts were initially created – medicinal sea-water cures – only this time packaged in a fancy building.

The Imperial Hydro at St Annes was built largely as a result of the enthusiasm of Oliver William Porritt, the son of W. J. Porritt, one of the founding fathers of the town. He commissioned architects J. D. & S. J. Mould of Bury, Manchester and London, to design the hotel, which was positioned on the 'prime site' in the town, at the corner of St Annes Road West and the North Promenade. According to the original prospectus published in the *St Annes on Sea Express* in February 1908, the scheme was for 'the erection of a palatial hydro hotel in the Renaissance style [combining] all the best features of the finest English and Continental spa hydros . . . included are hydropathic baths . . . a handsome and spacious ballroom and

theatre, 143 bedrooms . . . [and] a flat roof laid out as Winter Gardens, planted with trees and a bandstand'.[1]

Certainly the scheme was an impressive one and at first hand it seems difficult to appreciate why the proposals met with numerous objections from the good people of St Annes. After all, St Annes had only three main hotels in 1908: the St Annes Hotel, the Grand and the Victoria; all some considerable distance from the proposed site. What is more, the town could only have benefited from further guest accommodation; the population had grown from 4,224 in 1897 to 10,250 in 1908, the estimated summer population being 30,000.

There were criticisms of the scheme, however, and these seemed to be centred around two very strong themes; a powerful objection to another alcohol licence, and connected with that, the possibility that the hotel might attract the 'wrong type' of holidaymaker to the town. Objectors apparently believed seriously that a licensed hotel in the position of the hydro would attract the howling mob of holidaymakers of Blackpool. Miss Fulstow, co-principal of St Annes High School, was 'afraid if they granted a full licence it would be a serious attraction to trippers from Blackpool and loafers and undesirables',[2] whilst Edwin Cooper from the Drive Wesleyan Church was frightened that St Annes would become a 'halfway house' drinking place between Blackpool and Lytham.

This desire to be completely dissociated from its very commercial neighbour says a great deal about the attitudes of the St Annes residents at the time. Blackpool had become very popular

4896, THE BOATING POOL & HOTEL MAJESTIC, ST ANNES-ON-SEA

St Annes' impressive Imperial Hydro, later called the Majestic, came to symbolise the town's affluence. From hydropathic establishment it became, in turn, a military hospital, a nightclub, a broadcasting centre, government offices and a gambling club. The building was demolished in 1975, and flats which were built on the site commemorate the name 'Majestic'.

by the turn of the century, particularly with the working classes who, freed from the rigours of factory life for a week or so, looked for cheap lodgings and entertainment. Now reasonably successful in its own right, after struggling in the early years, St Annes wanted to maintain the same exclusive image as Lytham enjoyed. In reality, of course, the Imperial Hydro Hotel, when it was built a year later, helped to perpetuate that image rather than diminish it, due to its high prices and strict rules. Whether this was due to its lack of a licence – Porritt was denied one by the courts – is questionable. It seems certain that, licensed or not, 'the brawling masses of Blackpool' would not have been welcome at the hydro.

From the start, the hydro was advertised as an exclusive hotel for the well-heeled visitor. According to a 1915 brochure, the ballroom, a central feature, was 70ft x 38ft with seating accommodation for 600 people. The hotel included five floors and 120 bedrooms, each fitted with telephone, electric light and hot and cold water. There were electric elevators to all floors. This was quite something in 1915. Lawn tennis and croquet courts as well as quoits and dancing were publicised amusements; a ladies' orchestra played daily in the lounge and the hotel employed a resident lady entertainer. All this was quite apart from the water spas and health treatments; it was clearly a large-scale concern and an asset to the town.

The cures themselves look comical, if not sinister, today, and were aimed very definitely at the wealthy. As well as

The impressive and ornate ballroom at the Imperial Hydro. With seating for 600 people, it was a central feature of the establishment in its early days. By the 1920s it had become the most important attraction for the hotel, playing host to radio broadcasts of big band sounds.

treating breathing problems with Turkish baths, and sprains with a steam jet from the Russian bath, other more complicated apparatus was used for less obvious ailments. The Bergonie apparatus, for example, claimed to alleviate obesity or corpulence: 'Usually bright and cheery, the victims of this disease are often dispirited, irritable and subject to various stagnations in the nervous system, but by far the most serious effect is upon other acute diseases which are always most unfavourably influenced'.[3] The Bergonie machine took the form of a reclining chair fitted with electrodes of varying size, which were placed on the patient's thighs, arms and abdomen, and a small electrical current was sent through them to 'massage away the fatty tissue'.[4] Although appearing primitive now, the machine was not unlike battery-operated pads which are advertised today. Other machines included the Schnee 4-cell bath which was claimed to be 'the most important and most valuable advance in the history of electro-therapeutics'.[5] This treatment could be 'applied fifty different ways and had the great advantage that patients need not undress in order to use it'.[6] In 1915, a session of the Schnee Bath cost 3s. 6d. for residents, 4s. 0d. for non-residents. 'Radiant' heat was also used as the answer to lumbago and associated diseases. A horrible-sounding 'intra nasal' treatment aided various neuroses.

Interestingly, an X–Ray machine was part of the hydro's equipment. Available only to residents, X–Ray photographs cost a staggering one guinea each – a huge amount of money for the time. In its earliest days, the Hydro helped to substantiate St Annes' claim to be a 'watering place' again, rather than a holiday resort for pleasure seekers. It actually managed to attain a licence in 1922, after paying £2,000 for the privilege and promising to limit drinking to the drinking, smoke and billiard rooms.

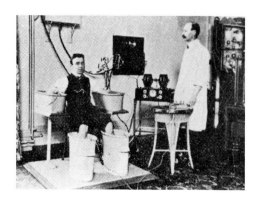

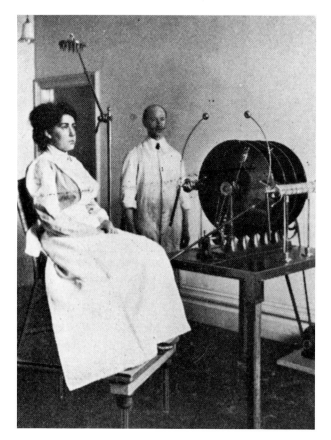

Above left: D'Arsonal High Frequency Apparatus being used for Auto Conduction treatment at the Imperial Hydro. Many of the machines were claimed to work by passing electric currents through the body, to treat illnesses as diverse as obesity and gout.

Above right: Dr Schnee's 4-cell bath. According to the Imperial Hydro brochure of 1915, this treatment could be 'applied fifty different ways and had the great advantage that patients need not undress in order to use it'.

Left: The Giaffe Static Machine. Many of the electrical treatments appear comical, if not positively sinister.

In the First World War, the hydro was requisitioned as a military hospital. After the war, water cures had become unfashionable and on 20 February 1920, the hotel dropped the word 'hydro' from its title, calling itself simply the 'Imperial'. Later that year, it changed its name completely to the 'Majestic', and a new image for the establishment was sought. Cleverly, the management used the still impressive ballroom to attract a different clientele to the hotel. Regular radio shows, featuring 'Geraldo's' (Gerald Bright) orchestra were broadcast from there. The hotel enjoyed its heyday in the 1920s and '30s, but due to the Second World War, this was not to last. During this war, it was requisitioned once again, this time for use by government departments. After the war, it was opened once again as a hotel, by James Brennan, but sadly its popularity did not return. The wealthy were now travelling abroad for their holidays and dance bands were becoming a thing of the past. In 1962 it became the Hotel Majestic Sporting Club; a gambling casino. This too was unsuccessful and marked the beginning of the end for the building. In 1975, the hotel was demolished to make way for luxury flats, still bearing the name 'Majestic' today.

Looking back at photographs of the Imperial Hydro/Majestic, the awesome presence seems to stand as a symbol of the wealth and prestige of the town.

1. *St Annes on the Sea Express*, 7 Feb. 1908, p. 2.
2. *St Annes on the Sea Express*, 19 Feb. 1908, p. 5.
3. Imperial Hydro Brochure, 1915, p. 39.
4. Ibid, p. 40.
5. Ibid, p. 36.
6. Ibid, p. 36.

All the Way to Lytham: the creation of the tramway

The history of the Fylde Coast tramways gives us an insight into the attitudes towards tourism in Lytham and St Annes at the time. Those attitudes are still to be found today. Blackpool pushes on regardless, shamelessly searching for new ways to entice the holidaymaker to its shores. Its trams are an important feature of its promenade front. Lytham St Annes, on the other hand, chooses its tourists a little more carefully and the trams are no longer used

to promote the town. Looking back, the reluctance to transport merrymakers from Blackpool to Lytham and St Annes can be seen as one of the reasons for the decline of the tramways in those towns.

At the end of the 1870s, just a couple of years after the creation of St Annes, proposals were made for a tramway along the Fylde coast. At the time, the pioneers of the new town were hungry to attract both new residents and holidaymakers and considered several propositions. There is

A tram running along Stoney Hill (Squires Gate Lane). The photograph shows the barren terrain which the trams were obliged to negotiate in the early 1900s; often they were left stranded when strong winds blew sand across the tracks.

Tram on Church Road, Lytham, almost at the end of its route from Blackpool South Shore. The tracks continued to Dicconson Terrace, opposite the pier at Lytham, and later along Clifton Street and Warton Street to the Cottage Hospital.

Two Lytham trams at Blackpool South Shore Station, the terminus of the Lytham to Blackpool route.

St. Annes-on-the-Sea

The tram route went right past the massive Imperial Hydro Hotel in St Annes Square. Objectors to the Hydro complained that its proximity to the route would encourage the 'day trippers from Blackpool and loafers and undesirables'.

little doubt that the tram route was built between Blackpool and Lytham partly as a result of the development of new St Annes. Equally, there is little doubt that St Annes, and more significantly, Ansdell and Fairhaven, progressed and prospered as a result of the tramway.

The first tramway on the Fylde coast was a two-mile electric conduit line on Blackpool Promenade, opened in September 1885. By 1895 Blackpool Corporation had developed their routes by constructing a double track from the Manchester Hotel along Lytham Road to Station Road, Blackpool, and as a result of this the St Annes and Lytham scheme was promoted. The British Gas Traction Company Limited obtained a lease for the operation of the St Annes section, opened on 11 July 1896. The new tramway began at the Station Road terminus in Blackpool, ran down Squires Gate Lane (then known as Stoney Hill) and along what is now

Clifton Drive North. It was mainly a single track with passing places. Tram sheds were built on Stoney Hill. According to D. F. Phillips in his article *Tramways of Lytham St Annes*,[1] at a lunch in honour of the opening, Mr Fletcher Moulton Q.C., a director of the British Gas Traction Company, pointed out that 'It only needed a good system of communication to make Lytham, St Annes and Blackpool into one continuous resort'[2] – an interesting statement, considering that only ten or so years later the last thing that Lytham and St Annes wanted was an association with Blackpool, but then it was in the Company's interests to see such a development.

An early obstacle facing the British Gas Traction Company was Blackpool Corporation's unwillingness to let Lytham's and St Annes' trams run on their tracks. It was Blackpool which refused to see the advantage of trips to neighbouring

The Blackpool, Lytham & St Annes Tramways Company tram on Clifton Drive, St Annes, in about 1911.

towns, and wanted to keep the ticket money from the trams for themselves. Perhaps they felt that Blackpool was already a big enough attraction and that people would be prepared to change trams to get there if they had to. Perhaps they wanted to reduce the competitiveness of the smaller resorts and this was one way of doing so. Whatever the reasons, passengers had to change trams at the Lytham Road South Shore terminus in order to carry on into Blackpool. Blackpool Corporation's own trams continued the journey. Since the South Promenade at Blackpool was not yet built, this was the only route by public transport that was readily available.

By 1901, the tramways were in the hands of the Electric Tramways Construction & Maintenance Company Limited, and it was they who carried out plans for electrification of the line. The new electrified tramtracks were opened on 28 May 1903, and stretched from Blackpool South Shore Railway Station to Clifton Square in Lytham. An extension along Clifton and Warton Street in Lytham was opened in September 1903.

In 1919, St Annes U.D.C. bought the tramways for £132,279. The trams' livery was changed to a 'discreet blue and ivory and, in accordance with the genteel atmosphere of St Annes and Lytham, windows of the saloon cars continued to be hung with curtains . . . the wooden seats of cars one to twenty were furnished with strips of turkey red carpet'.[3] By now, St Annes and Lytham were no longer bothered about being isolated from Blackpool; in fact they heartily encouraged it. These towns had become very fussy about the kind of visitor they wanted to attract and this was reflected in their policies towards the tramways. At a meeting of ratepayers to approve the purchase of the tramways by St Annes U.D.C., Councillor E. Lee emphasized the feelings of many St Annes residents when he maintained that 'the Council wished to be masters in their own house. They did not want either Blackpool, or a private

Tram running along Clifton Drive, Ansdell. There is no doubt that Ansdell and Fairhaven, as well as St Annes, developed and prospered as a result of the service.

company, or anyone else, pouring passengers into the town just when and how they liked, without consulting St Annes' interests. It was always a problem in St Annes how far they should cater for the respective claims of residents and visitors and what type of visitors they should encourage'.[4] He added that while 'they must never overlook the claims of the toiling masses of Lancashire for a reasonably free access to this delightful part of the coast . . . he did insist that St Annes Council should be the authority to consider and determine the position on that matter'. St Annes U.D.C., in effect, bought the tramway to prevent parties they may have considered undesirable from getting their hands on it, rather than as a potentially commercial concern. This was a complete reversal of attitude from Moulton's assessment in 1896. In fact, the amalgamation of Lytham and St Annes in 1922, just three years after St Annes U.D.C. paid out, was primarily an attempt by the towns to dissociate themselves

completely from Blackpool. Certainly, St Annes, at least, saw itself emerging as a different type of resort from Blackpool and wanted to make that point clear to everyone, including the 'toiling masses of Lancashire'.

Once St Annes U.D.C. realised that it no longer wished the town to be linked to Blackpool, the end of tramways in Lytham and St Annes was on the cards. In 1923, just one year after the amalgamation, the first motor buses were bought to run alongside the trams. Although 'there was considerable opposition from many of the elderly retired residents in the Borough, who complained that they were unable to hear the approach of a bus as they formerly could a tram . . . and were compelled to leave their residences for the bus stop much earlier than had been necessary in tramway days',[5] the buses did prove to be more popular than trams, not least because of the number of breakdowns experienced by trams, due largely to sand blowing across Clifton Drive from the sandhills and blocking the tracks – something which was less of a problem in Blackpool. Severe gales in December 1929 required the use of buses alone, when trams literally became stranded on the rails. By early 1936, the motor bus fleet had been increased to twenty-three and by the end of that year the tram service between Lytham and St Annes had been completely taken over by the bus service. The Squires Gate to St Annes service ceased a year later.

The tram tracks in Lytham and St Annes were taken away very soon after the cessation of the service. Whereas Blackpool and Fleetwood maintained their service, by and large, as a tourist attraction, Lytham St Annes deliberately shunned the trams. This further emphasized the separateness of the twin towns – they were definitely *not* part of Blackpool.

1. Donald F. Phillips, 'Tramways of Lytham St Annes', *The Tramway Review*, vol. 2; no. 14, 1954.
2. Ibid, p. 107.
3. Ibid, p. 115.
4. *St Annes on the Sea Express*, 9 Jan. 1920, p. 5.
5. Phillips, *Tramways*, p. 125.

Piers and Pierrots

Today, piers epitomise British holiday resorts. Entertainments and amusements have been associated with them since the 1860s. Before that, they were merely landing stages for boats bringing in tourists by sea. Some were established with commerce in mind – jetties for the offloading of goods. When coastal resorts were made accessible to the working and middle classes by the development of the railways, these landing stages were adapted into pleasure piers complete with amusements for the new visitors.

The development of a pier at Lytham seems to have been something of an aberration for the town, bearing in mind the air of gentility and graciousness that it was striving to maintain. Dr Poole, writing in 1909, emphasized that the town was 'one of those places which does not cater for the day tripper and is rapidly becoming a fashionable residential watering place'.[1] Why then, aware that the very nature of a seaside resort attracts visitors from inland, seeking sun and sea, did the people of Lytham promote more of this activity by building a pier?

It is possible that Lytham, despite its desire to remain aloof from the brawling commercialism of 'boisterous and bracing Blackpool',[2] wanted to thwart its neighbour's attempts to be the first resort on the Fylde coast to boast a pier. The Lytham Pier Company Ltd. actually applied for a pier in 1861, but Blackpool pipped them at the post by building what is now the North Pier in 1863. The first pile of the Lytham pier was only placed in 1864.

The pier, constructed on clusters of cylindrical iron columns, began at a point on the esplanade opposite Dicconson Terrace, and extended seaward 900 feet. It was designed by E. Birch, and cost £5,890, becoming renowned for its elegant balustradings and iron work, and its expensive gas lamps. Lady Eleanor Clifton opened the pier on 17 April 1865, amid much ceremony. Special trains ran from Bolton, Manchester and Preston, and the town was treated to a procession as well as a display by the Lytham lifeboat crew.

The pier was designed for gentle strolling – almost as an extension of the promenade. Seats were placed on each side of the pier along its entire length, for those who tired and wanted to sit awhile in the sun. However, the pier company also promoted steamer trips to other resorts – Southport and Blackpool – and also to Preston. An ornamental house was included on the pier, as a waiting room for those embarking and disembarking from the ships. The pier was not free: it cost 2d. to walk on the pier, 6d. for every bath or sedan chair, 4d. for a perambulator. For steamer passengers the rates were steeper: from 6d. for anyone landing at the jetty to a very expensive £1 0s. 0d. for any shipmaster going to or from his own vessel. There was even a baggage handling charge, between 2d. and 3d. depending on weight.

Although the Lythamers were content for the pier to be run as a commercial venture, the less genteel entertainments associated with piers at the time – vulgar song and dance acts and open-air concerts – were not encouraged. The pavilion was only added to the pier in 1892, as part of alterations costing £12,000. Even then, it only offered the mildest of amusements – orchestral concerts, dramatic light opera

Lytham Pier, with the passenger steamer sailing out to sea. The pavilion was not added until 1892, when the whole pier was reconstructed at a cost of £12,000.

and musical comedy performances. In the summer music festivals were held. Not here did one find the naïve pierrots as at St Annes or the bawdy side shows and machines of the Blackpool piers. It was almost as if Lytham was embarrassed by its sea-front attraction and tried its best to keep it low key.

The decline of the pier can perhaps be traced back to the apathy of these early times. In 1903, £1,400 was spent on restoration work after the pier was almost sliced in two when two barges were driven through it in strong gales. In 1928 the pavilion, which had been used by then as a cinema, was destroyed by fire, and despite a £12,000 design by Alderman Arnold England, was never rebuilt. This was the start of a long period of neglect which finally necessitated the demolition of the structure. In 1945 the new owners of the site, Lytham Pier and Amusements Ltd., put forward a hugely ambitious scheme to convert the pier into the shape of a ship; the plans included workshops, a large

restaurant with a window view of the coast, amusement arcades, roofdeck for sunbathing and an observation platform designed like the bridge of a liner. So adventurous were the plans that the roofdeck was to have dividing screens, in the shape of boat sails, to meet changes in wind direction and so provide shelter for the sunbathers. Not surprisingly, the scheme never got off the ground, money for these luxuries not being plentiful at the end of the Second World War. It is hard to believe that such a gigantic and obtrusive development would have been acceptable to the residents of the town.

In the early 1950s the owner, Mrs Nellie Kamiya, wanted to demolish the weatherbeaten and rusty seaward end and develop the rest, but to no avail. Towards the end of the decade the council had lost patience with what it now regarded as an embarrassing eyesore and, wanting to improve its foreshore, decided to rid the town of the structure. Demolition started on 4 March 1960. Obviously, a pier at

St Annes pier, looking towards the town. So popular did the pier become in the early 1900s that the management employed ushers to keep the crowds moving and to avoid queues building up on the busier days.

St Annes pier looking towards the sea, in about 1915. The impressive Moorish Pavilion, built in 1903, can be seen on the right, and on the left is the Floral Hall, opened in 1910, where concerts were given by the Pier Orchestra.

In 1903 gale force winds drove two barges against the pier, slicing it in half. The cost of repairs amounted to £1,400. Only eleven years earlier, £12,000 had been spent on the reconstruction of the pier, and some of its renowned ornamental ironwork can be seen in this photograph.

Lytham was no longer necessary; Lytham was moving away from its holiday image.

St Annes was still in its infancy when the decision to build a pier was taken by the Land & Building Company in 1879. Apart from St Annes Church and the newly built St Annes Hotel, there were no other public buildings. The early construction of a pier shows that from its earliest days, St Annes was being developed with the tourist industry in mind. The pier, designed by A. Dowson, was opened by Lord Stanley on 15 June, 1885. If the opening day was anything to go by, it seemed that St Annes would take as its example the Blackpool piers, rather than the sedate pace of Lytham's. The place was chock-a-block with bootblacks, sweet vendors, Aunt Sallies, coconut shies, Punch and Judy shows. A local report claimed that the 'promenade was a spectacle which St Annes had never witnessed before – from the pier entrance to the extreme end towards the lighthouse – it was one long array of hawkers and other claimants upon the visitor's purse'.[3]

In its early years, the pier structure was very basic. It was 315 yards long and seven yards wide, and had ten recesses (not shelters) at intervals along its length, with seats. At the end of the pier there was enough space for open-air entertainment with seating for an audience, and an elevated bandstand. The jetty for steamer passengers extended 30 yards or so beyond the pier.

Taking a walk along the pier became a fashionable pastime for those of the wealthy middle class who wanted to improve their health. Despite this it seems

The pier was very basic in its early days. The present-day entrance was not built until 1899, and the Moorish Pavilion and Floral Hall were added in 1903 and 1910 respectively. Alderman Cocker, Mayor of Blackpool, commented that 'they were not going to satisfy people merely with seats', but, in the beginning, the jetty for passenger steamers and the seats were the pier's only attractions.

that the pier was not over successful in its early years – hardly surprising when it consisted solely of a waiting area and seats. Alderman Cocker of Blackpool commented that 'they were not going to satisfy people merely with seats'.[4] There was an obvious need to extend the pier and increase its facilities. A new entrance was added in 1899, and in 1903 the entire structure was doubled in width and a Moorish-style pavilion, seating 75 people, added. This Moorish pavilion witnessed the beginnings of the fashion of St Annes for entertainment by pierrots and minstrels. These enjoyed immense popularity with both tourists and residents and were instrumental in increasing the success of St Annes Pier. At the height of its popularity, pier managers were known to hire ushers on Sundays to keep crowds moving along the pier and to minimise queues, so busy had it become. Perhaps the most successful entertainer was Freddie Carlton. He came

to the town in the early 1900s, after travelling as an entertainer around the world. He left after working on the pier in his first summer season, but returned with his own company, the 'White Coons', a year later.

Their act, combining the talents of music hall type entertainers, magicians, singers and dancers, was successful for nine seasons on the pier. Feeling the need to organise his own shows, though, Freddie moved his company in 1909 and established his own 'Cosy Corner'. Using only a crude stage built into the sandhills opposite Riley Avenue, these outdoor performances were exceptionally popular. He was a particular favourite of children and, as 'Cousin Freddie', encouraged them to sing, dance and act by organising talent competitions. In bad weather, Carlton took his show to the public hall, later the Palace Cinema, in Garden Street to perform.

A large audience on St Annes Pier, watching one of the shows – possibly Freddie Carlton's company 'The White Coons'.

Freddie Carlton's makeshift outdoor theatre, on the beach opposite Riley Avenue, where his 'music hall' acts gained him a successful reputation with residents and visitors.

Freddie Carlton, creator of 'Carlton's Cosy Corner'. After nine years performing on St Annes Pier with his company 'The White Coons' he established his own outdoor theatre on the sandhills.

In 1911 Carlton's open-air theatre was replaced by a grand new pavilion, the 'Cosy Corner Pavilion', designed by Albert Winstanley. Perhaps aping the pier's 'Moorish Pavilion', it too was built in Moorish ornamental style with domes and was equipped with 'all modern conveniences, including electric light and fire hydrants'. A sliding canvas roof covered the structure so that it could be opened in hot weather and sliding windows were included, no doubt to capture the feeling of being 'outdoors' like the original 'Cosy Corner'. It accommodated 1,700 people, a considerable number – the pier's pavilion seated only a maximum of 1,000.

Perhaps to counter the individual success of Freddie Carlton, and to give the town another type of entertainment, a Floral Hall was constructed on the pier in 1910. This was for entertainment of a more genteel nature. It had seating for over 800,

In the early days, the Pier Orchestra performing at the Floral Hall was all-female. The first male conductor, William Rees, took over in 1934. Employed to bring a more genteel and refined atmosphere to the pier, the orchestra's morning and afternoon concerts were popular with gentlefolk.

and many orchestral concerts were held there, often during the day. The early Pier Orchestras were all female; not until 1934 did the first male conductor, William Rees, take over. Between the end of the Second World War and 1966, Lionel Johns became the pier conductor; his programmes were often broadcast on national radio and were a tremendous boost to the popularity of the pier.

Over the years, many famous acts have appeared – Bob Monkhouse, George Formby and Tommy Trinder being just three – as well as less familiar ones such as the Rossendale Clog Dancers. But towards the late 1960s the pier was struggling to maintain its reputation. A disastrous fire in June 1974 gutted the Moorish Pavilion; in 1983 the Floral Hall was also destroyed in the same way. Money was not available to return the pier to its former glory. It is unlikely anyway, given the change in people's tastes in entertainment, that it would have repeated its previous successes. The pier structure still exists, though, and its magnificent entrance reminds us of its illustrious past.

1. Dr Poole, *Lytham* (Corporation Guide series, 1909).
2. Ibid.
3. *Lytham St Annes Express*, 14 June 1935, p. 12.
4. *Blackpool Gazette and News & Fleetwood, St Annes & Fylde News*, 19 June 1885, p. 9.

The Gardens of the Fylde: improving the outlook

As the holiday trades developed in Lytham and St Annes, a series of Improvement Acts was passed by each town, as a result of which further facilities were created or converted for use by visitors. It is interesting to note that the Acts passed by both towns expressed a desire to please the residents as well as attract the tourists.

Sea fronts and promenades, naturally, are important to every holiday resort. Lytham and St Annes used theirs to reflect the atmosphere of their towns. Whilst Blackpool and similar places allowed tradespeople to tout their wares and entertainers to parade their acts along their sea fronts, Lytham and St Annes managed to keep their promenades for promenading, and select promenading at that. The promenade was adapted to emphasize the wealth of the resort.

The 1847 Lytham Improvement Act gently hinted at the improvements which could be made to the town, with sanitation

Lytham Green in about 1900, popular even in Victorian times with children and picnickers. The windmill in the background, which was restored after a fire put a halt to the milling in 1919, has become the town's best-known landmark.

The promenade at Lytham. Free from stalls and bawdy entertainments, it was enjoyed as a place for strolling and sitting.

After the 1904 Lytham Improvement Act most amusements were restricted to the pier, the entrance to which can be seen to the right of this photograph. The promenade was left for 'promenaders', free from the funfair atmosphere that Blackpool chose to cultivate.

and roads taking precedence. The Improvement Act of 1904 went further by stating exactly what type of improvements were to be made. In many ways this Act influenced the character of Lytham. The promenade developments came under scrutiny, as the council was now empowered to regulate or prohibit the erection or placing on the seashore and the approaches to the beach of any booths or stands that might be considered for entertainment purposes. These included 'stalls (moveable or fixed), or vehicles for the sale or exposure of any article or thing or photographic carts or other vehicles

whether drawn or propelled by animals or persons and the playing of any games'.[1] This was a definite policy on the part of the council to avoid the 'tackiness' that Blackpool had begun to enjoy. All amusements were now to be limited to the pier. From this time Lytham began to focus its tourist policy on the walkways of the town, promoting the adage 'leafy Lytham' to suggest the greenness of the town, rather than its sea- and sun-bathing aspects. The council adapted the promenade to suit visitors who chose to take the sea air by walking on the front, rather than those seeking amusement there. Elegant seating

Lytham's Lowther Gardens, built on land originally known as 'Hungry Moor' because of its lack of vegetation. John Talbot Clifton presented the deeds of the ground to the council in 1905.

Ballam Road, an example of one of the many walkways that earned Lytham the name 'Leafy Lytham'. Cultivated with trees and shrubs, these walks emphasized the rural, rather than the coastal, aspect of the town.

and shelters were constructed in the hope that the visitors of quality would make use of it and in this way promote the town.

Until the 1840s sand dunes occupied the area on which the large green was eventually to be laid out, to become as much an attraction for the town as the beach. After the windmill, built in 1805 for milling corn, ceased to be used following a fire in 1919, it enjoyed a reputation as the town's most famous and distinctive landmark. The green has become synonymous with picnics and ballgames, and old photographs show that children made use of the area, even in the Victorian

days, for the same purpose.

Whereas contemporary resorts exploited the surrounding towns and villages for 'day trips', Lytham instead chose to publicise walks around its own town. Green Drive and Ballam Road were popular routes for walkers and cyclists; inland from the sea front, they provided a welcome variation from the 'typical' holiday activities and they attracted visitors very different from those at Blackpool. 'The walks are various and many for those who love exercise; the lazy will soon tire here – but the active will never be at a loss.'[2] An early snippet in the

Lytham Times says it all: 'Lytham has its charming walks and rich rural scenery and a quiet holiday can be enjoyed, there being none of the bustling excitement which is found at other much-frequented resorts . . . it is certainly the "beau ideal" of a resort for those who desire a quiet holiday near the sea, in the midst of charming scenery and far from the boisterous hilarity of the mad'ning crowd'.[3] No longer wishing to compete with brash Blackpool, Lytham was making use of its own more exclusive facilities.

Likewise, Lytham's select and elegant Lowther Gardens emphasized the superior social status of the town. Originally known as 'Hungry Moor', because of the poverty of the sandy soil, the twelve acres of land were presented to the council by John Talbot Clifton in 1905. They were named after Clifton's maternal grandfather,

Colonel Lowther, a well-known politician and sportsman, who died in 1868. There is no doubt that Clifton donated the gardens to Lytham in the hope that they would be an asset to attract visitors to the town. Although not a great advocate of change, he appreciated the need to develop Lytham if it was to compete commercially with the more successful Blackpool.

In fact, the gardens were never a tourist attraction. The pavilion which was added very much later was used by local amateur dramatic and operatic groups, and served a community-minded population instead. A bowling green and tennis courts were built with residents in mind and it became a popular area for local families. Even now, the high railings surrounding the land could perhaps be a little intimidating to the stranger. The gardens did not live up to John Talbot Clifton's expectations.

St Annes Promenade in about 1890. The stark landscape is broken only by the dramatic Lifeboat Memorial.

The children's paddling pool and a packed bandstand on St Annes Promenade.

A busy St Annes Promenade. The foreshore was developed with gardens, bandstand and, later, a miniature golf course and boating pool in an attempt to mix the 'genteel' air of the walkways of Lytham with just a little entertainment.

The new bandstand, built in 1908, was formed in the shape of an amphitheatre with seating on three raised tiers. The panels of the tiers were constructed from pebbles to give a 'coastal' look, and the sandhills still surrounded the structure on three sides.

The new esplanade of promenade gardens designed in 1914 as part of the St Annes on the Sea Improvement Act, and extending the full length of the promenade to Fairhaven Road.

Similarly, St Annes attempted to create a cultivated image with its promenades and gardens. An 1896 Improvement Act suggested the laying out of the promenade with some form of garden seating and allowed the council to enforce byelaws to discourage the erection of booths, tents, sheds and stands for the sale of articles and shows and exhibitions. The Act set a precedent for the 1904 Lytham Improvement Act. The town considered building a bandstand at about this time, although it was not actually constructed until 1908. The town was careful, even in the beginning, to attract a residential as well as seasonal populace, but the tourist industry was uppermost in the minds of the early entrepreneurs. By the turn of the century, however, attitudes had begun to change. St Annes U.D.C. was just as concerned with keeping its residents happy as with pandering to the requirements of holidaymakers. It is interesting to consider the reasons behind

the decision to build a bandstand, as they tell us a lot about the attitudes towards tourism by then. Early photographs of St Annes front show a very stark landscape, with only the Lifeboat Memorial standing out to break the monotony. The building of a bandstand was seen as a compromise: it was a tourist attraction in its own way, and it was acceptable to the townspeople as well. It was built in the form of an amphitheatre and provided seating for 1,200 people. More or less horseshoe-shaped in design, three terraces were constructed in concrete around the stand; single chairs were then secured to strips of wood along the terraces to provide the spectator accommodation. The panels surrounding the tiers were built with stone pebbles, which, according to a report at the time, lent 'a prettiness that well becomes a band kiosk by the sea'.[4]

The bandstand proved popular; as many as 2,000 persons assembled at some of the performances. Sunday performances

A waterfall and cascade, made to look 'as natural as possible', were the central feature of the new gardens. Between 300 and 400 gallons of water a minute were lifted by an electric pump to flow over the cascades, which operated from 10 a.m. to 10 p.m. in the holiday season.

were an innovation for August 1908, tactfully arranged around church services so as not to offend pious residents. It was quite a successful venture for the council – the townspeople liked it and so did those whose business interests lay in the holiday trade.

This early work was a sound basis for further development of the promenade at St Annes six years later. The St Annes on the Sea Improvement Act of 1914, unlike its predecessor of 1904, advocated positive policies towards tourism. It permitted the extension of the South Promenade at a cost of £2,600. An effort was made to preserve the natural features of the shore; marram grass and flowering gorse were included in the landscaping. Ornamental lakes with stepping stones were placed in the sandhills and there was an alpine garden with flowering shrubs. The central feature was a waterfall and cascade constructed of water-worn rock and made to look as natural as possible. Between 300 and 400

gallons of water per minute were lifted by an electric pump and sent from an upper lake, over the rocks down the cascade and into a lower lake, to be lifted again. The cost of running the fall in 1914 was 3d. to 4d. per hour, and it ran from 10 a.m. to 10 p.m. in the holiday season. It was illuminated at night, and soon became a major attraction. In building the rest of the gardens, nearly 1,000 tons of rock were used: 300 tons of weather-worn and 500 tons of Derbyshire and Clitheroe stone. The crazy footpath was fashioned from blue clay found under the peat on Marton Moss.

The new gardens were greeted with enthusiasm by residents and press alike: 'St Annes can now justifiably claim to have the prettiest esplanade in the country'.[5] There is no doubt that the gardens heralded the development of further projects in the town, particularly the open-air pool in 1916, and helped to create St Annes' reputation as the 'garden

Ashton Gardens were laid out to create the feeling of a 'garden' rather than of a 'park', and included as much natural scenery as possible, with rustic stonework and a lot of ornamental detail.

town' of the Fylde – no mean feat for a seaside resort! The residents approved because what had been a stark and barren outlook had been transformed into a pleasant walkway and sitting area. The managers of the Imperial Hydro and the Grand Hotels must have been rubbing their hands with glee at the improved views from their windows.

Twenty years later, the gardens were developed even further. A new St Annes foreshore scheme included plans for a children's boating pool, a miniature golf course and a new promenade walk, at a cost of £15,000.

Unlike Lytham, St Annes did want to develop some entertainments in the town, but definitely not on the same scale as Blackpool. Maintaining an air of grace with its beautiful garden surroundings, it did provide some facilities – a miniature golf course, boating pool and bandstand – and whilst not reaching the scale of the commerce of Blackpool, these gentle

entertainments did help the town to establish a personality of its own.

Although the promenade gardens are a significant focus for the town, the Ashton Gardens are better known. The original grounds, then known as St George's Gardens, were laid out in the first years of the town's existence, 1874–5, by Mr E. Thomas, a landscape gardener from Aughton. He was also responsible for building the promenade gardens as part of the 1914 improvement scheme.

St George's were ornamental gardens with a refreshment room at the entrance. Covering about twelve acres, they preserved as far as possible the natural sand dunes and became very popular with picnic parties when St Annes first began to grow as an alternative resort to Lytham and Blackpool. Not unexpectedly, the St Annes on the Sea Land and Building Company, through a subsidiary, controlled the grounds and managed them in the early days. In 1896, the Company offered to sell

The Rose Garden in Ashton Gardens. Over 6,000 rose bushes were planted when Lord Ashton bought the gardens for the council in 1914. Laid out essentially for the enjoyment of residents rather than visitors, the gardens became synonymous with the refined atmosphere that the town came to enjoy.

the gardens to the council for £12,000. The council, hesitant of increasing the rates for the venture, decided against the purchase, even though it was an ideal opportunity to renovate what had once been one of the town's most picturesque attractions.

The refusal to buy the gardens emphasized a decided slump in the fortunes of the town at that period. Having risen from the sand dunes to become a prosperous town, St Annes was experiencing anxiety over which road it should take next.

Should it continue to cater for the holidaymaker – its original aim after all – or to the needs of its now well-established residents? Eventually, W. J. Porritt took over the lease of the gardens, but in 1912 the council was again called upon to consider purchase when Porritt asked the Land & Building Company permission to build on the rest of it. It must be remembered that, at this time, St Annes Council was already committed to erecting

the new open-air pool as well as generally improving the promenade area. To take on another proposal would require an increase in rates for the townspeople. A poll to decide the issue was organised. Dramatically, on the eve of the poll (which was to be on 27 January 1914) Lord Ashton, the linoleum magnate from Lancaster, made voting unnecessary when he magnanimously donated £21,350 to the council for the purchase of the gardens. He contributed a further £4,526 to buy more land and to make improvements. Ashton's remarkable generosity seems inconceivable today. Apparently, after being sent anonymously two copies of the *St Annes Express* dealing with the controversy, he came forward with the money to spare the ratepayers the decision. Why he should have done this has never been fully explained: a generous benefactor in his home town, he had always shown a deep interest in the development of St Annes. In his letter to the council, accompanying the donation, he claimed that 'it would give him much pleasure to contribute to its prosperity and to the enjoyment of its residents and visitors'.[6]

The gardens were renamed the Ashton Gardens, and were developed along traditional lines. An old English rose garden – over 6,000 rose trees were planted – and a rock and water garden, designed by Pulham & Sons of London, were central features. In addition, thirteen tennis courts were provided – as well as a large bowling green – these definitely with the residents, rather than the visitors, in mind. The gardens were officially opened on 1 July 1916, by Councillor R. Leigh.

Later, the gardens were extended to 14½ acres and the Ashton Pavilion was erected. Once again this catered primarily for the requirements of St Annes residents. Suggested originally as a band pavilion on columns, its sides fitted with lattice work for summer use only, it was developed into a hall to be used for the benefit of local people and visitors alike. In the winter, residents organised concerts and dances. Amateur drama and music societies performed in the elegant structure, which was also used as a theatre. A fire in March 1931 caused £1,300 worth of damage, and a second fire in September 1977 destroyed it almost completely. Despite public support for rebuilding, this has never happened.

The gardens are still a focal point of the town and local people make extensive use of them. To visitors, however, they are perhaps not so well known.

1. *St Annes on the Sea Improvement Act*, 1904
2. P. Whittle, *Marina*, p. 28.
3. *Lytham Times*, 10 April 1897, p. 5.
4. *St Annes on the Sea Express*, 10 June 1908, p. 5.
5. *St Annes on the Sea Express*, 29 May 1914, p. 9.
6. *St Annes on the Sea Express*, 30 June 1916, p. 6.

In the Swim: indoor and outdoor pools

The enthusiasm for bathing was not confined to the sea. Resorts were also expected to have swimming baths. Lytham was no exception. It had baths at least as early as 1814, and in 1863 the building which housed the swimming baths also provided upper and lower assembly rooms, the upper room holding a stage. The western portion was until 1894 rented by Mr S. Wartenberg as a store for antiques and *objets d'art*. It was known as 'The Parisian Bazaar'.

Mixed bathing was not permitted; originally there were separate pools for men and women. A 71-year-old resident, reminiscing in 1964 about the old pool, remembered an adjacent hall where plays and concerts were performed. It is generally thought that Lytham's first cinema was also here, but there is no substantial evidence for this.

The Lytham Baths were entirely rebuilt between 1926 and 1928. The original assembly halls were extensively altered and modernized, and pool and assembly rooms reopened on 9 June 1928. Like the fashionable Imperial Hydro at St Annes, hydropathic treatments were offered to attract wealthy tourists. The opening brochure claimed the baths to be

The original Lytham Baths, opened in 1863. Part of the building was rented by Mr Wartenberg and housed an antiques store, 'The Parisian Bazaar'.

'amongst the finest in the North of England; and unique in that they are amongst the only remedial baths in the North where hot and cold water baths may be obtained'.[1] The promotion was directed at those potential clients who were looking for health and beauty treatments. The baths proudly claimed that 'sea water is today accepted as one of the best media for the treatment of rheumatism, sciatica, gout and allied ailments', and offered such remedies as 'a special cabinet for bronchial treatments', 'Pombiere Intestinal Laval treatment for cases of colitis, constipation, toxaemia etc.', 'Russian Vapour Baths' and 'Mustard, Sulphur and Pine Baths' as well as Turkish Baths and the usual plunge pools. The brochure pointed out that 'Health is indispensable to complete happiness, and the new remedial baths at Lytham have been provided by the Corporation to enable you to keep your

health or to restore it to you if you are ill'. It was important for the council to show that the new baths were for the residents as well as the tourists.

Whilst the baths at Lytham emphasize health treatments, St Annes' open-air pool was a place to have fun and be seen in. One of St Annes' greatest attractions was its open-air pool, opened in 1916. Built at a cost of £10,000, the baths were 240ft x 120ft, and contained 820,000 gallons of filtered sea water. The buildings were designed in what was regarded at the time as 'simple Renaissance style', by Fred Harrison, architect, of Accrington and St Annes. In later years, it became known as the 'Roman Bath', swimmers associating its majestic columns around the pool with the Roman era.

Aware that by then St Annes was enjoying a reputation as an exclusive holiday place, catering for a privileged and

The new Lytham Baths, opened in 1928. Constructed of sand-faced brick and Stancliffe Stone dressings, they were of Georgian design to 'harmonize with the architectural character of Lytham'.

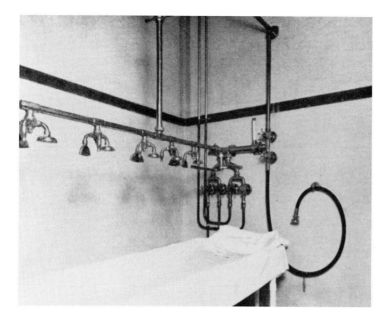

The management claimed that Lytham Baths were equipped with 'fittings throughout of the finest quality approved by the medical faculty; no justifiable expense having been spared by the Corporation to offer the most efficient hydropathic treatment to a wide and critical clientele'.

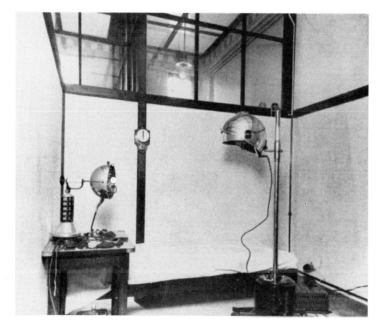

The baths' ultra-violet ray treatment lamp. 'The radiations act beneficially in two ways, firstly by increasing the bactericidal power of the blood, and secondly, by activating the vitamins of the body.'

wealthy minority, the council took great pains to retain an atmosphere of respectability. The buildings, although finished in concrete and cement plaster, were 'so arranged as to form little obstruction to the seaward view from the Promenade',[2] with flower beds and a rockery laid out as an approach to the pool. The changing cabins contained dressing tables and mirrors, and hot water for footbaths. What is more, music was provided for spectators by a ladies' orchestra. Obviously, this was not the place for a quick ten lengths and out; it was the setting for polite society.

Accommodation for spectators was a wide expanse of terraced seating for

An early photograph of St Annes open-air pool, showing its popularity. There are more people spectating than swimming; special seating for the 'thousands' of visitors was included in the original design.

several thousand. The early success of the baths is evident from photographs at the time which show large numbers of people, both in the pool and sitting or walking along the sides. The flat roofs of the building were formed into balconies and promenades. At a much later date these were used for sunbathing, but in the 1920s and 1930s they were very popular with people just strolling and taking in the air. A luxuriously furnished cafe, 33ft x 16ft, completed the complex.

The cost of entry to the baths, in its first years, depended on the age of bather and the time of day. For adults it cost 3d. before 9 a.m. and after 5.30 p.m., but 6d. between those times. Children under sixteen paid 2d., rising to 4d. Sunday bathing was at the higher rate. Season and family tickets were available for 15s. 0d. and 12s. 6d. respectively, and a swimming lesson cost 1s. for twenty minutes. Promenaders were not exempt either: 2d. per visit, or 7s. 6d. for a season ticket. The

The high diving board and water chute at the open air baths. Promenaders paid 2d. per head for the privilege of strolling on the balconied walkways adapted from the flat roofs of the outside buildings.

baths were certainly a valuable source of income.

The pool retained its popularity for many years, the managers being very much aware of the need to adapt facilities as fashion changes. Several attractions were included in programmes for the baths, among them Professor Stearne, an accomplished Channel swimmer, who in 1916 and 1917 gave exhibitions of long-distance swimming and such feats as 'feeding whilst in the water'. There were life-saving displays and exhibits of 'ornamental swimming' by the local lady swimmers. Managers showed foresight in adapting the baths to suit the times; the promenades became sunbathing spots, the cafe opened with entertainment in the evenings and in the 1950s modern and old time dancing was arranged in the daytime too.

Gradually, fashion dictated the decline of the open-air pool. People demanded more modern swimming facilities. Lytham baths, too, were coming to the end of an era, and maintenance of both was proving excessively costly. A new indoor pool was opened in 1987, supposedly to replace both the outdoor pool and Lytham's indoor one. For a while the open-air pool continued to attract custom, despite the lack of heating, but the cost of remaining open for a dwindling number of die-hard swimmers was too great and it was closed in 1988.

Optimistically, some hoped that the pool might be saved as a commercial venture and restored to its former glory, but in 1992 the pool was demolished and replaced by 'St Annes Pleasure Island', a £250,000 project including a splash pool, water slides and water-based attractions. At least the original intentions have been maintained – water for residents and, perhaps more significantly this time, the holidaymakers, to enjoy.

It is possible to look back and admire the courage of the men of the council in 1916. Building the baths was a very ambitious project at that time. Their success is a testament to their foresight. The baths' decline was inevitable as people's expectations changed and the money to adapt to that change was unavailable. It was cheaper to build anew.

1. *Souvenir Programme of the opening of Lytham St Annes Corporation Baths, 1928,* p. 5.
2. *Open Air Roman Baths official opening souvenir, 1916,* p. 5.

A Game for the Wealthy: golf in Lytham and St Annes

'It is not necessary at this day to plead the virtues of golf, which as everyone knows, re-transforms business-worn shadows and jaded politicians into rosy-faced, genial mortals, who can really enjoy a good dinner.'

Brochure for the Imperial Hydro, 1915.

The game of golf has become closely linked with Lytham St Annes. It was introduced to the area soon after the birth of St Annes by Alexander H. Doleman, a Scotsman resident in South Shore, Blackpool, who became known as the 'father' of Fylde golf. Golf originated in Scotland and Doleman practised the sport on the sand dunes fringing the shore just outside Blackpool. He eventually attracted interested parties who came to watch him play. He had been unsuccessful in his attempts to promote the game in Blackpool, but St Annes was another matter. Several prominent St Annes and Lytham dignitaries expressed an interest and at a meeting held at the St Annes Hotel a decision was made to start the Lytham and St Annes Golf Club. The meeting took place on 27 February 1886 and besides the enthusiastic Doleman, eighteen other men were present, including Thomas Fair, agent to the Clifton estate, J. Mugliston, one of the first club captains (known as 'Uncle John'), the Rev. W. G. Terry, A. Wykeham Clifton of Warton Hall – great uncle of John Talbot Clifton of Lytham Hall – and Lieutenant Colonel C. Addison Birley, all important and wealthy men in their own fields and all influential in developing the Fylde. Other famous names who joined the original nineteen in their first year were Charles Macara, W. J. Porritt and Alderman William Henry Cocker. The Lytham and St Annes Golf Club was officially opened on 6 March 1886. The game was for the wealthy: those who joined the club in its early days were those who could afford to take time out to play during the daytime. It was regarded as an exclusive club for gentlemen; all the early members were gentry or men of professional standing. It is certainly true that their eagerness was instrumental in the development not just of the game in the area, but of St Annes as a town as well. The club was an important factor in the transformation of the sand dunes into valuable land. In addition, wealthy residents were attracted to the town, from other parts of the country, to the golf course. In turn, wealthy holidaymakers also took time out to visit the course. It was a very big attraction and still plays an important part in the image of Lytham St Annes as a resort for richer folk.

The first course was situated on the 'other side of St Annes', that is, north of the railway station. A part of the original links is now within the boundaries of what is today the Old Links Golf Club. Other tees and fairways are now covered with streets and houses. George Lowe, the first professional golfer hired by the club, used a wooden shack, situated where Oxford Avenue is today, for his caddy house and locker room. The club continued to use the St Annes Hotel as its headquarters: a room was allocated to them by the proprietor, A. J. Holloway.

42337. ST. ANNES-ON-SEA: GOLF LINKS.

Golfers playing on the new Lytham and St Annes course in about 1910. The clubhouse in the background was designed to the requirements of club members by Woolfall & Eccles of Liverpool. The club was obliged to move from its old course between St Annes Road and what is now Highbury Road, and the new links opened in 1897. They hosted the British Open for the first time in 1926, and since then have played a prominent part in British golf.

The plentiful sand on the course, together with the tough grass that bound it together, made it a testing one and from its early days it attracted some of the best players in the country. The first competition was held only a couple of weeks after the formation of the club, in April 1886, but was for club members only. Handicaps ranged from –30 through scratch to +17, the +17 being given to Doleman. J. Mugliston won with a round of 123, reduced to 98; J. Marcus Rae was second. Doleman with his heavy handicap only managed third place with a net 109.

The first Open or 'Strangers' competition was held on 26 March the following year. John Ball had the lowest score, with 73 shots, but his handicap of +11 raised his total to 84. As a result, a club member, W. H. Harrison won with 94 shots reduced to 76. The Open was a great advertisement for the club and for the town. Visitors travelled from all over the north of England to play and watch the game.

Later, too, ladies were able to enjoy golf on the course. The first ladies' Open Championship was held in 1893, and won by Lady Margaret Scott. A report of the time remarked 'Lady Margaret appeared in the field with her grand style and beautiful swing, the length and accuracy of her shots, together with the perfect ease – free from all signs of force – with which she extricated herself from any difficulty . . . revealed what ladies golf could and should be'.[1] The fashionable game appealed to women of the upper and middle classes and the club seized upon this opportunity to promote themselves further by attracting lady players as well as men. Lady Margaret won £50 first prize, a sizeable amount for the times.

The opening of the new clubhouse on the Old Links Course, May 1911. Costing approximately
£6,000, the clubhouse replaced the previous wooden pavilion.

The club moved to its present location in 1897. John Mugliston, on becoming captain in 1890, had attempted, unsuccessfully, to obtain permanent tenancy of the golf club's land from the St Annes on Sea Land and Building Company. The company had fixed their priorities on renting for building purposes, however, and would only concede a portion of the land. St Annes had become so busy, due in no small part to the development of golf in the area, that the land was needed for housing. From then on, new premises were sought by the members. The club approached the Clifton estate as early as 1890 for land between St Annes and Fairhaven; negotiations continued over the next six years. Members wanted better facilities for their club, with changing rooms and comfortable surroundings. They were prepared to put forward money themselves, but not while the tenancy remained temporary.

The new links were ready in 1897. The clubhouse was designed by Messrs Woolfall & Eccles of Liverpool to members' specifications. Even before the clubhouse was completed, competitions were played on the new course. The old links continued to be used until the tenancy was terminated in early 1898. The new clubhouse fulfilled the highest expectations of the members, with luxurious settings; 'a steward was appointed and the club included a serving bar, club room, billiards room, a large dining room, ladies' accommodation and workshop for the professional'.[2] It reaffirmed that golf was a rich man's sport. In 1926 the club played host to the British Open, a prestigious honour which it has repeated since, giving Lytham St Annes a major place in the history of British golf.

The success of the Lytham and St Annes Golf Club encouraged the development of other clubs in the vicinity. Fairhaven Golf Club was formed in 1895. In its earliest days, the course was laid out in the narrow area between Fairhaven Lake and the inner and outer promenades. A connecting wooden bridge allowed access over the stream. The clubhouse was what is now the Lakeside Cafe. The club was obliged to change its location three times before it acquired its present site. The original low ground course was partly washed away after a particularly high tide and the members moved to higher ground on the seaward side of Clifton Drive. The new clubhouse was a pair of semi-detached houses on St Paul's Avenue, the first tee being immediately opposite what is now King Edward VII School playing fields. When further building was planned on the site the club came to an agreement with the Clifton estate to lease the present ground in Lytham Hall Park. The new links were laid out by club architect, J. A. Steer, acting under the advice of James Braid. The club has increased its popularity over the years, celebrating its golden jubilee in 1975.

The Old Links Golf Club, standing largely on the old site of the Lytham and St Annes Golf Course, was established in 1901, just three years after the Lytham and St Annes members were removed from the site. Green Drive Golf Club, on the edge of Lytham itself, was opened in May 1913, on 80 acres of land offered by John Talbot Clifton. The original links were laid out by eminent golf architect Dr MacKernie.

By 1913, four major courses existed between Lytham and St Annes, with a total membership of over 1,800. Not surprisingly, the tone of the resort was strongly influenced by the game, an expensive pastime. This guaranteed that a large number of residents and holidaymakers had the money to keep the resorts select.

1. A. M. Starkie–Bence, 'Golf for Ladies', *The Lady's Realm* (1896), p. 88–9.
2. E. A. Nickson, *Lytham Century* (Nickson, 1985), pp. 26–7.

A Promising Resort: the development of Fairhaven

'What more delightful pleasure can there be when the fierce sun oppresses with his fiery rays than 'gliding like happiness away' on the rippling water, fanned by the zephyrs of the west?'

Advertisement feature on Fairhaven Lake from the St Annes on the Sea Express, *15 July 1904.*

Described by Barrett's 1907 directory as a 'promising resort, situated between Lytham and St Annes',[1] Fairhaven is the newest of the Fylde's coastal towns. Like St Annes, it was developed largely as a result of the enterprise of one man – in this case Thomas Riley of Fleetwood. As Hargreaves had done a few years earlier in St Annes, he envisaged a new ideal watering place. In 1892 he formed the Fairhaven Estate Company which, as the St Annes on the Sea Land and Building Company had done, leased land from the Clifton estate.

The lease allowed the company to take gravel from the large deposits in the district for road making, and this was a significant factor in the rapid development of the town. Although initially the company planned to erect a pier, early building was of a residential nature. By 1896, 43 residences and shops had been established but only one hotel. Later the emphasis was placed on the construction of the marine lake, around which nearly all Fairhaven's future tourist attractions developed.

The lake had a maximum depth of 3ft 6ins., and was 11 acres in extent. It was decided early on that pleasure boats would be the main attraction for Fairhaven, and in 1908, 60 rowing and sailing boats were available for hire on the lake. In July 1908 a portion of the lake was marked out for swimmers, forming an open-air marine pool within the boating lake. A swimming club was established just a month later. The original plans for the lake area included a marine drive about two miles long for promenading and driving. This was semi-circular and overlooked the open sea. A large piece of land was also reserved for cricket and tennis. To advertise the benefits of the lake to residents, boating regattas were introduced in 1899. Other activities included obstacle racing in and out of the water, swimming demonstrations, life-saving exhibitions and events such as scaling the greasy pole across part of the lake, the unlucky participant falling into the water much to the amusement of spectators.

The resort prospered but was not developed much further by the Fairhaven Estate Company. In 1923, what had been developed was acquired from the company by Lord Ashton of Lancaster at a cost of £34,000. Once again, this generous man had intervened in the fortunes of the Fylde coast. The Ashton Marine Park, as the area became known, was presented to the town in the same year. It was officially opened by Lord Derby on 7 May 1926. The newly acquired park was part of a larger scheme which would cover 100 acres, much of it still sandhills. The plan for the area was prepared by Messrs T. H. Mawson & Sons of Lancaster and London and included an extension of the existing lake and the creation of a central pavilion called a 'Kursaal', a popular contemporary term, to

Nr. Lytham. Fairhaven Lake.

The Wrench Series, No. 4257.

Two views of Fairhaven Lake around the turn of the century. Although ambitious plans for the Ashton Marine Park included a Kursaal to house dancing, concerts and exhibitions, a 'popular refreshment house' was its only major building.

accommodate dancing, concerts, exhibitions and restaurants. A promenade was to be installed in front of the Kursaal in the form of an amphitheatre with formal ponds and a bandstand. Provision was made for bird sanctuaries, further tennis and croquet courts, and an 18-hole miniature golf course as well as an 18-hole pitch and putt course and an open-air theatre. An enclave for sea lions was even considered. Needless to say, only a few of these schemes actually came to fruition. In Barrett's Directory of 1934, improvements are mentioned; additional tennis courts and bowling greens are given particular attention, but the larger undertakings did not materialise.

The comparative failure of the 1926 plans was Fairhaven's salvation. It meant that the resort was not opened up as a larger commercial concern, but remained as it was originally intended by Riley, a pleasant area offering safe boating recreation only.

1. Barrett's *Directory of Preston and Fylde Districts* (1907), p. 756.

In Conclusion

Much has happened to change our attitudes towards holidaying in Britain's coastal resorts. With cheaper air fares making foreign locations more accessible, these pleasure havens of the past are no longer fashionable.

In many ways, both Lytham and St Annes have moved away from the holiday industry. The main purpose of the local council is now to serve the residents. Occasionally, a gesture towards the holidaymaker is noticeable; the current development of the old open-air pool site into a sports leisure complex at St Annes is being constructed partly as a tourist attraction. The same can be said for the introduction of jet skis to Fairhaven Lake, a cause of extreme annoyance to the residents there.

Many of the buildings erected for the holiday industry in Lytham and St Annes no longer exist – the Imperial Hydro and Lytham Pier, for example. Others have been adapted for a different use. Lytham Baths and Assembly Rooms now house rooms for local organisations and societies. The gardens are used as much, if not more, by the townspeople as by the visitors, and of course, the golf courses are very exclusive. A glimpse into the holiday past is rare, St Annes Pier and Bandstand are two of the last vestiges of the tourism of yesteryear. For the rest, we are left only with photographs.

The reluctance of Lytham and St Annes to attain the role of holiday resort in the past has left its mark on both towns today. The elegant streets and buildings have survived because of the requirements of the people who live there. While Blackpool and similar resorts have gone overboard in indulging the less exclusive tourist, perhaps at the expense of the residents, the initial reluctance of Lytham and St Annes to develop along these lines has been their saving grace. The charm and graciousness of these towns will continue for years to come.

Bibliography

Adamson, *S. H., Seaside Piers* (Batsford, 1977).

Anderson, J., and Swinglehurst, E., *The Victorian and Edwardian Seaside* (Country Life Books, 1978).

Ashton, Ed, *Lytham* (printed by Mather Bros., 1946).

Bainbridge, Cyril, *Pavilions on the Sea* (Robert Hale, 1986).

Baines, Edward, *History, Directory and Gazetteer of the County Palatine of Lancaster*, vol. 2 (Wales & Co., 1825).

Collins, Herbert C., *Lancashire Plain and Seaboard* (Dent, 1953).

Harrison, Gabriel, *Rage of Sand: the Story of the Men who Built their Own Seaside Town* (Ernest Benn, 1971).

Howell, Sarah, *The Seaside* (Cassell & Collier, 1974).

Moorhouse, Sydney, *Holiday Lancashire* (Robert Hale, 1955).

Motor Age Lytham: a Proposal by Lytham St Annes Civic Society (Civic Society, 1965).

Nickson, E. A., *The Lytham Century: a History of Royal Lytham and St Annes Golf Club, 1886-1986* (Nickson, 1985).

Phillips, Donald F., 'Tramways of Lytham St Annes', *The Tramway Review*. vol. 2, no. 14 (1954).

Pomfret, Tom, 'Story of Lytham St Annes', *Lytham St Annes Express*, 16 Oct. 1958.

Poole, Dr, *Lytham* (Corporation Guide Series, London, 1909).

Porter, John, *The History of the Fylde in Lancashire* (1876, reprinted by S. R. Publishing Ltd., 1968).

Searle, Muriel, *Bathing Machines and Bloomers* (Midas Books, 1977).

Starkie–Bence, A. M., 'Golf for Ladies'. *The Lady's Realm* (1896), pp.87–90.

Walvin, James, *Beside the Seaside: a Social History of the Popular Seaside Holiday* (Allen Lane, 1978).

Whittle, P., *Marina: or an Historical and Descriptive Account of Southport, Lytham and Blackpool* (Author, n.d.).